Feeding  Pediatrician's Guide to Happy and Healthy Mealtimes.

I cannot guarantee that your children will learn to eat healthily. This book aims to show you recent research and current thinking on the subject. It aims to provide parents with the best tools and the most stress free way to achieve such a result.

Dedication

This book is dedicated to my beautiful and wonderful family, especially to my children and husband. Without you my life would be incomplete.

Feeding Toodlers. A Pediatrician's Guide to Happy and Healthy Mealtimes.

Dr Orlena Kerek, pediatric doctor and mother of 4 shows you the stress free way to healthy happy meals for picky, fussy or otherwise toddlers. (For the sake of argument, all toddlers are considered fussy!)

Contents

Introduction

Becoming a parent is one of the most exciting and terrifying things that can happen to you. I love being a parent. I love being a mother to my four amazing children. I love watching my four beautiful children grow and learn and enjoy life.

So why terrifying? Parenting is tough and it's easy to have doubts about the things that we do. As parents we want our kids to grow up to be happy and well rounded people who will enjoy life and be healthy. But what if we are doing it all wrong? What if we're actually teaching them to be horrible people who will be miserable and unhealthy?

I'll let you into a secret.

There is no ONE right way to parent your kids. There are better ways to connect with your kids, to teach them things, to be a parent, to enjoy family life. But we are all different and what works for one child or family, won't work for another.

We have to find our own way and we will ALWAYS be racked with doubts.

Not only are we worried that we aren't good enough, the day to day parenting can get really tough at times, especially during those toddler years.

Believe me, I know, I have toddler twins.

Toddlers can be SO exasperating. They ask for a blue cup. You cordially give them the blue cup. They throw it back at you in disgust.

Every single part of the toddler day is challenging and frustrating. We struggle to get them dressed, out of the door, in the bath, and out of the bath again and into bed.

Toddlers don't like to do things the easy way.

Or quickly.

And meal times. Did I mention mealtimes?

My toddlers shout and scream and then shout some more at breakfast, lunch and dinner.

It makes feeding them difficult and I haven't even started on the "healthy bit" yet.

My healthy broccoli, carrots, sweet corn, apple. Yep, those lovely healthy fruit and vegetables go flying across the room.

I'm well trained at ducking missiles.

But.

I want my kids to grow up not just eating, but LOVING healthy food.

In this book, I'm going to show you the easiest and most stress free way to teach your toddler healthy eating. Please note that I said 'most stress free' not 'entirely stress free'. We're talking toddlers here and as far as I can work out they don't do 'entirely stress free'.

But I will show you how to help them eat a healthy diet so that YOU won't be stressed about that. You will know that you are doing everything you can to feed them healthy food and to teach them healthy eating habits that will stay with them for life.

You may well be wondering who I am and how on earth I can the utter the words "healthy eating and toddler" in the same sentence.

My name is Orlena (or Dr Kerek, if we're going to be formal.) I'm from the UK (so please excuse the British spellings, we like extra vowels, they aren't typos!) where I trained as a doctor and worked as a paediatric doctor. Then in 2011 I moved to Spain and started writing about how to help children eat healthily.

It didn't happen exactly like that.

I had children, and then realised how incredibly difficult it was to get them to eat anything green. How they would wolf down an entire packet of biscuits and leave their healthy dinner untouched.

So I read all the theory about how to get them to eat their veggies. I changed the way I did things. I stopped saying things like "yeah! welcome to the clean plate club," and "if you eat one mouthful of spinach you can have a sweetie!"

Then I started writing about it.

Healthy eating is something I'm hugely passionate about as I know that we have an epidemic of obesity and poor eating. I know all the horrible and nasty disease that you are more likely to get if you eat a bad diet.

And I know that if we can teach our kids to eat healthily and to genuinely love healthy food, they will carry on those habits into adulthood and have much much lower chances of all those horrible diseases such as diabetes and even some cancers.

They will be given the best chance that we can give them of a healthy life. (We can't guarantee anything in life, but we can do our best to work the statistics in our favour.)

The Proof Is In The Pudding

My children do not eat a perfect diet and they have never ever tried a bit of kale. (Actually I can't buy it here but I've heard that it's great for you.)

But.

They eat a diet that I am happy with. They eat lots of fresh fruit and vegetables. My three year old daughter eats lettuce from the salad bowl. Her twin will eat a whole plate of broccoli. My 8 year old (the fussy one) has even started eating uncooked tomatoes. A year ago he wouldn't touch them.

There are lots of things that they don't eat. My oldest son especially has a long list of things he never ever eats. Eggplant (aubergine), mushrooms and fish are at the top of his "I don't eat that" list.

And they love ice cream and candy and chocolate. They would happily eat ice cream every single day. And in the hot summer months we often do. Sometimes we eat shop bought "not at all healthy" ice cream and sometimes we eat delicious homemade frozen yogurt made with just frozen fruit and yoghurt. No added anything. Sometimes it's fruit popsicles. Or fruit popsicles AND ice cream. (It gets really hot here in the summer.)

They are still learning to love healthy food but overall their diet is great. Despite the shouts and screams at mealtimes, I am not stressed or worried about what they consume.

Lots of people have told me that my methods have helped them. I don't want to bore you with a billion quotes so I've picked the two that I think illustrate how easy it is to feed your toddler a healthy diet when you know how.

"One of my 2½ year old twins is an extremely picky eater, and I am trying to help him learn to eat a variety of healthy foods. Your approach is so positive and not overwhelming that it really feels like something I can do!"

"We are always trying to make sure that our children eat healthy and that even in our absence they should be able to make better choices themselves. I found your book perfect!"

My Promise

I promise that if you follow this guide you will see amazing changes in your children's diet. If you keep a food diary now and another in a year's time, you will be astounded at the difference you have made.

I also promise you that if you teach your children to eat a healthy diet, that they will be in the best possible place to lead a healthy and active life. You will give them the best chance possible to live to a ripe old age with the least amount of illness possible.

You will also stop being worried and stressed at mealtimes because you'll know that you are doing everything you can to help your kids.

So let's find out what's wrong with the clean plate club and delve into the secrets of hassle free healthy eating for toddlers.

Let's start by looking at exactly why toddlers are so challenging and why feeding them is so stressful (that's feeding them in general, not just healthy food.)

Chapter 1. The Problems with Toddlers

Let's start by finding out exactly why toddlers have challenging behaviour in general and how this makes feeding them a healthy diet especially difficult.

"I love you!" Sebastian says as he covers me in sloppy wet kisses. "I love Daddy and Galen and Dante and Celeste. I love everyone!"

I love toddlers. I love the way they are so cute. I love the way they talk. I love their chubby little hands and their sloppy kisses and sticky cuddles.

Which is just as well really because like the movie "Gremlins" that cute little teddy is apt to transform into a monster. One minute they're all happy and singing. The next they are hollering at the top of their voices as if the world was coming to an end. Apparently they are asking for a biscuit.

If it weren't for their redeeming cute features we'd have to change that common phrase and turn the baby AND the toddler out with the bath water.

There is no doubt about it.

Toddlers have challenging behaviour.

We'll discuss why this is in a little bit. For now, let's look at toddler eating.

Babies are Good Eaters

Most parents are more worried about introducing solids than feeding their toddler. It seems like a challenging and strange time.

But once you've worked out the basics, most babies are actually very good at eating and exploring new foods and tastes. That "mouthing" reflex, when they shove everything into their mouth comes in handy if you're trying to encourage them to grab a stick of broccoli and eat it.

Parents think that they have got the hang of the whole eating thing and settle into a comfortable routine, looking forward to the next toddler challenge.

Little do they expect that it's going to be eating again.

Out of the blue, their little baby turns into a toddler and instead of shovelling everything into their mouths, they start to refuse foods that they once enjoyed. They start flinging food all over the place and they start screaming and shouting.

That is not an easy combination for parents to deal with.

My Toddler Challenges

Each of my children have had their share of meal time traumas. My son who is now three is especially challenging.

He will start to shout "I don't like it!" even before he has seen what is for dinner. (That is one of the most frustrating things when kids refuse to try something that you know they would like if only they gave it half a chance.)

He shouts and screams and shouts some more. Sometimes he gets so upset that he will throw his cutlery and knock over his chair.

When he calms down, he has entirely forgotten what he was upset about. He'll suddenly look at his plate and start eating the offending meal.

"Yum! I like this don't I?" He says.

Next meal, chances are we have to go through the whole rigmarole again.

I have no idea **exactly** why he gets upset. But it doesn't really matter.

The best way to deal with his behaviour is with patience and persistence. Persistence in feeding him healthy food.

Why are Toddlers So Challenging?

There are many reasons why toddlers are challenging. They are at a particularly "delicate" developmental stage. They are leaving their baby-ness behind and they think they are growing into a big boy or girl.

But it doesn't happen overnight.

They know what they want but they can't express it. Even if your toddler is really good at talking (and the majority aren't) they still don't have the ability to express their thoughts eloquently.

Sometimes their thoughts don't even make sense and they don't actually know what they want. They asked for a blue cup. You gave them a blue cup so why are they still shouting?

Toddlers are very loud, very good at screaming and not very gentle. It's not unusual for toddlers to thump and hit, pinch and bite. Sometime they do it because they're angry but at other times it's just being boisterous. Ever had a toddler run up to you enthusiastically and ram their head into your legs? Or give you a "love smack in the face"?

They just haven't learnt that it hurts or that you perceive it as pain.

Adrenaline Overload

Toddlers are very governed by the primitive part of the brain (commonly referred to as the "limbic system") that triggers the "flight or fight response".

When you are scared, your body triggers it's survival mode. There are three options available. Fight (shout and scream), flight (run away) or freeze like a rabbit in the head light.

When this happens, your body is surging with adrenaline, a powerful hormone that makes your heart rate go up.

As we grow older we learn to control that part of our brain more. We learn to tell ourselves that the perceived danger isn't really danger and we find ways to calm ourselves down.

Toddlers are very good at triggering the response and not so great at calming themselves. (Although some may find ways of calming themselves with things like sucking their thumbs or having a favourite teddy.)

Once that response is triggered, you can't just hand them a blue cup and expect them to stop screaming. Their heart is still pounding and flooded with adrenaline. It doesn't just turn off because you've "solved the problem".

Toddlers Can Do Anything

Or so they think. Especially if they have older brothers or sisters.

They just don't get that their 8 year old brother is perfectly capable of scooting down the hill, swimming out to sea or even walking to school ALL by himself. (We live in a very quiet Spanish town and live 2 whole minutes from school.)

They don't understand they aren't 8 and just haven't developed all the skills that their older siblings have.

There is No Rush

They also don't understand the concept of time. Or doing things quickly. They are perfectly happy to spend all morning getting dressed. Or just not bother.

When you want to leave the house, they decide they want to examine a crack in the road for half an hour.

Or when they DO decide that they're going to do it by themselves, they have to do it 30 times. Just to make sure.

Taste Buds Change

And to top it all, their taste buds change. They may genuinely NOT like something that they ate as a baby. My oldest son used to eat bananas like they were going out of fashion. Now he won't touch them. He can smell them a mile off.

He didn't have a bad experience. Something just changed and he stopped liking them.

But that doesn't mean that they don't like everything that they claim not to. (We'll discuss that later in the "Solution" chapter.)

A Normal Toddler

So there you have it. A "normal toddler" is a little person who shouts, screams, throws things, hurts you, and refuses to do anything you want them to.

And to top it all off, they take their time to do the things they've decided they actually want to do.

It is lucky that they are so cute otherwise I suspect the human race would have died out a long time ago!

Life Is Frustrating

It is frustrating being a toddler. It is also frustrating looking after a toddler.

As much as we love our gorgeous toddlers, there is no doubt that having someone scream and shout at you all day and refuse to do the menial things in life like getting dressed and brushing your teeth is wearing.

Parents want a quiet life. Or at least I do.

So it's hardly surprising that when toddlers shout and scream about the food you have just spent hours making, you feel fed up and wonder why you bother.

Why go to the effort of cooking food that they're just going to throw back at you?

In an attempt to avert the tantrums, parents give toddlers what they think they'll want to eat. Normally this is something that isn't particularly healthy.

And as they complain about more and more things, their diet gets narrower and narrower. Until one day you realise that your toddler only ever eats macaroni cheese.

Or in my case, I found my toddler crying on the toilet because his poo was painful. He was constipated because he wasn't eating enough fruit and vegetables. Even though I was giving him what I thought was lots of vegetables. I thought I was feeding him a healthy diet.

That was when I realised that it wasn't as easy as I had thought to get your toddler to eat healthy food.

In Summary

All of this challenging behaviour combines to make life with toddlers stressful and hard work. Parents and toddlers have two different agendas and to make life bearable, the first thing that gives is healthy eating.

Eating habits get worse and worse until you realise that you've slid down a slippery slope and are standing at the bottom of a huge mountain that you don't know how to climb.

But don't worry, I'm going to show you the solution to getting your child to eat a healthy diet. Of course I can't magic away all those normal endearing toddler characteristics, but I can show you the best way to go about teaching them healthy eating habits.

Before we think about your toddler and what food you're going to give them, let's have a look at your stress levels and how we can help you feel calmer and more relaxed about your child's diet.

Chapter 2. Let Go of the Stress

Before we get into the nitty gritty of "how" there is one thing I want to explain to you. I want to show you how to let go of the stress that is surrounding your child's diet. I want to show you how to let go of all that worry and concern that your toddler is not eating broccoli.

Ease Off the Pressure

Even if you presented your kids with the most perfect, well balanced healthy diet, chances are that they would not **consume** a perfect, healthy well balanced diet.

You cannot force your children to eat the food that they are presented with. You cannot prize open their mouths and tip the peas and carrots in and think that is healthy eating.

In fact, evidence shows that even pressuring your children to eat has negative consequences. Pressuring your kids to eat can lead to things like bulimia and eating disorders.

Pressuring your children to eat normally (but not always) leads to the **opposite** effect. The more you tell them to eat something, the less likely they are to give it a go.

Pressuring your kid to eat includes saying things like "you can't have dessert until you've finished your main course" or even "just try one bite".

It also includes any reference to the out-lawed "Clean Plate Club".

I know it is tempting. (Please believe me I know EXACTLY how tempting it is. I have to force myself not to say these things on a daily basis.)

But we aren't going to do it.

We are simply going to present the healthy food and allow our children to decide what they want to eat because we want to teach them to enjoy healthy food, not to eat it because they have someone pointing a metaphorical gun at their head.

But this chapter is titled "let go of the stress" how exactly does that work?

You need to change your mindset a little for this to work, but bear with me.

How to Relax

Step 1. You no longer need to shout at/encourage/persuade your child. Feels better already doesn't it?

Step 2. If it is new, they won't eat it.

Introducing new foods to kids is a large subject, for now let's keep it simple. Kids don't "like" what they don't know. In order to get to know something they have to try it **at least 15 times** (roughly). When it is familiar they MAY decide to like it. On the other hand they may decide they don't.

So "I don't like it" includes all things they don't like plus all the things that haven't truly made their mind up about. Plus if you're a toddler, "just because it Tuesday" will do. There is no rhyme nor reason.

So now you don't have to persuade them to eat the food plus you don't expect them to eat new foods. So don't even bother trying. How are your stress levels doing? Much better?

Step 3. You have time on your side.

The Benefits of Healthy Eating

Why do we want our kids to eat a healthy diet? Because there are a whole host of amazing health benefits. You are less likely to get cancer, you're highly unlikely to be obese (there are a few genetic causes of obesity but they are rare), they are much less likely to get type 2 diabetes which has horrible side effects and is a leading cause of death. Less likely to get heart disease.

The list goes on. In short, it is definitely worth putting in the effort to teach kids healthy eating habits, which by the way, develop at a young age.

Eating habits develop as young as 3 years old so teaching your toddler to eat healthy is great. (If you have older children, don't worry, you can change habits, it's just if you get in there early it's much easier.)

Step 4. Think of Childhood as a 'Training Ground'.

What About Child Health?

Yes, child health is important too although those BIG benefits happen later on in adulthood.

It is of course worth eating healthily in childhood to avoid childhood illnesses such as constipation due to not eating enough vegetables. Constipation in childhood is actually very common and normally related to a poor diet.

But.

There are other things that you can do in the short run. (I would start with lots of prunes, hiding vegetables in sauces and if that didn't work, go visit my doctor.)

If You are Worried Go to Your Doctor

If you are worried that your child's diet is so bad that it is affecting their health or their growth, go to your doctor. If their poo is not soft like squidgy ice cream or they have pain when they go to the toilet, go to your doctor. Or you just want a second opinion, then you should go and see your doctor.

They will tell you if there is a problem (in which case you have cause to be worried, but it still won't actually help). If not you can relax and let go of the stress.

Of course you still need to work at healthy eating. Just without worrying about it.

Step 5. Let Go of the Individual Meal

If You're Not Worried, You Don't Need to Stress

If you just want to teach your kids to eat a healthy diet for all those great benefits then you can let go of worrying about that individual meal. It doesn't matter if they eat that one pea or that one carrot.

Because.

Firstly, you'll be offering them healthy food throughout the day (that's coming up) and they'll probably have already eaten some fruit and vegetables before refusing the pea.

But secondly, it doesn't matter. Your aim is to teach them to love and choose healthy food, not eat it under duress.

And that doesn't happen overnight. It is a skill that they have to learn. They will, it will just take time.

Stress Free

How's your blood pressure now?

OK, I know. I have 4 young kids and life with kids is never stress free, especially if one or more of them is a toddler. Not only that but those doubts will creep back. You will find yourself telling your children to try a bite, to encourage them to eat, to tell them how very tasty the broccoli is.

That is normal. Just remember and stop.

Remember that you are teaching your child to choose healthy food and you are doing it with the least amount of stress possible.

In Summary

As long as your child is in good health, you can let go of all the stress surrounding healthy eating because most of the big buck benefits happen later on in life. At the moment you are teaching them to love healthy food.

You are also not going to pressure them to eat because you know that it doesn't work in the long run and suddenly you'll find that mealtimes are no longer a battle ground. If your kid doesn't want to eat, that's fine.

You are now calm and relaxed about your kid's diet because you know that you are doing everything you can to teach them healthy eating. You are actually doing those things. You are enjoying it and so are they.

Hang on a sec? What things? We'll get to that in a bit. Firstly, if we want our kids to eat a healthy diet, we'd better check that we know exactly what a healthy diet is. No point in going to all this effort and teaching them how to eat junk.

Chapter 3. What is Healthy Eating?

Teaching your toddler to eat healthy food has two main criteria. Firstly you need to present them with a **healthy diet**. And to do that, you need to know exactly what a healthy diet is. That's what we're going to look at in this chapter. (Don't worry, it's not too in-depth or complicated.)

The second aspect to healthy eating is how you present that food throughout the day, your "healthy eating routine". We'll get to that in the next chapter.

Mostly Vegetables

There are many different ideas of what is the "ideal" diet. They all differ on various points but there is one indisputable fact.

Vegetables are good for you.

Not only are vegetables good for you, but the majority of people don't eat enough vegetables and they don't even realise it.

I'm going to go with the US "My Plate" guide as it is easy to understand and I think it is sound advice.

Here's the thing.

50% of what you eat should be fruit and vegetables. A little more vegetables than fruit.

Seriously! Most people are surprised when they realise how much fruit and vegetables they should be consuming.

Toddlers Love Fruit

I suspect that your child doesn't eat that much. I also suspect that if they do eat any fruit and vegetables, they prefer fruit to vegetables.

That's fine. Kids prefer the natural sweetness of fruit and tend to prefer it to many vegetables.

Just keep presenting the vegetables and remember that fruit is far better for you than packaged food.

Grains

Around 25% of what you eat should be grains. That's things like pasta, rice, bread. All those things that are high in carbohydrates.

Lots of kids like carbohydrates. I fondly refer to 2 of my kids as "carb junkies".

It is better to let them eat healthy unrefined carbohydrates such as pasta, rice and wholemeal bread rather than cookies and cakes. Or prepackaged foods.

If your child is a carb junkie, keep presenting the fruit and vegetables. Try to encourage the healthy options rather than restrict their intake. (Although of course, you can restrict the amount that you present. For example, you could give them a small square of bread with lots of vegetables rather than let them have free range of the bread basket.)

Whole Grains

Whole grains are grains that haven't had the outer husk removed (or less of the outer husk removed.) The husk is where all the fibre is and fibre is good for us (it's the bit that stops up from being constipated and has other benefits.)

Fibre is a substance that our bodies don't digest, it just passes through us but we still need to eat it. Consuming sufficient fibre is the basis of a healthy diet. Fibre is found in fruit, vegetable and whole grains.

It is recommended that half of the grains that we eat are wholegrain. That's brown stuff, so brown bread and flour, brown rice. You can even get whole grain pasta these days.

Protein

Around 25% of what you eat should be protein. Protein is the stuff we are made up of. The "building blocks" of the body. It is found in meat, eggs, fish. There are also some great vegetable sources such as garbanzo beans (aka chick peas) and other legumes.

Meat sources of protein are called "complete proteins". Your body can make most of the 25 amino acids (the bits that proteins are made from) by itself but there are 9 "essential amino acids" that it can't make. We need to get these amino acids from our diet. If a protein contains all 9 in sufficient quantities, it is called a "complete protein". Most vegetable sources aren't "complete" but can be combined with another vegetable source to give you all 9 essential amino acids. Rice and beans is a good example of combining vegetable sources of proteins to give you all the amino acids that you can't make.

Red Meat and Packaged Meats

I recommend restricting the amount of red meat that you eat as it has been linked to bowel cancer. Red meat includes dark meats such as beef, lamb and pork. White meat is lighter and includes chicken and turkey.

All packaged meats are included in this restriction (whether they are white or red, so sliced turkey is included.)

The link is not entirely clear but the main culprits that cause cancer are suspected to be "haem" which is part of the red blood cell (red meat is red because it has more blood in it than white meat) or nitrates that they use to package meats, whether they are white or red.

Non Meat Proteins

I think that eggs are a very healthy, economic and tasty complete protein. And that lentils and garbanzo beans are cheap and tasty and underused by most people.

Fish

Fish is a very healthy source of protein and has added health benefits (and helps your brain function well.) Most people don't eat enough fish. Aim for at least 2 portions a week.

Dairy

Dairy products such as milk, cheese and yoghurt are a little portion that sits on the side of MyPlate but are not included in the actual plate. They are a source of calcium which is very important, especially for growing bones.

It is perfectly possible to get calcium from other sources if you don't want your child to eat dairy products. (I would recommend talking to your doctor or dietician before eliminating it for any reason.)

Fats

Fats come in different forms. Animal fats are normally solid at room temperature whereas plant fats are normally liquid at room temperature and are called oils.

Fat has been given bad press in recent years but it is now thought that fat isn't as bad for as we were previously advised.

I like to cook with olive oil. (I live on the Mediterranean coast, it's what's available here which is lucky for me.)

A little bit of animal fat is fine, but I would encourage you to use a plant oil that is naturally unsaturated as your main cooking oil. The less processed the better.

Drink Water

Water is the best drink for us all. It is great at quenching our thirst. All other drinks should be drunk in moderation. Even fruit juice which is delicious and reasonably healthy still contains far far more sugar than water by itself.

Fizzy water and caffeine free infusions (with no added honey) are a great alternative to water if you like a change. I love to make tea from mint, fennel leaves, a piece of lemon or ginger. Once they are cooled, toddlers can drink them too.

Children also like water with a piece of fruit or cucumber in it. Beware of bottled 'flavoured water' that might be soda in disguise. Check the label to see if it contains more ingredients than water and whatever flavour it has added.

Empty Calories

These sound good don't they? But in fact, it means foods that are very high in calories but have no nutritional benefit. Foods such as added sugar and fat fall into this category.

Interestingly the US MyPlate includes cheese in its list of empty calories. But you are allowed some empty calories so don't despair if your child is a cheese loving monster!

Less Packet Food

Nowadays, the choice of packaged food available is overwhelming. It is so easy and so convenient just to reach into the cupboard and pull out a packet of something that you know your kids will eat.

But.

There's a big but. Processed food is exactly that. Processed.

They often take out the good nutrients and replace them with bad ones. (They want them to last longer on the shelves so they take out the tasty stuff and then they have to replace it with artificial flavours.)

They are high in added sugar, salt, not-great fats and other things that we don't know how to pronounce.

If you think that you can't survive without any packet food, I'm sure you'll be able to cut down on the worst.

Look at the labels and actually read what is in the food that you buy. (If you don't recognise it, that's a bad sign. Look for ingredients you understand.)

Look for packets with less ingredients. You want yoghurt that says "yoghurt" rather than a list of 30 things you've never heard of before.

Nothing Is Forbidden In Moderation

It may sound as if you have to live off broccoli and kale forever and never get to enjoy the sweet treats in life. But actually, if you eat a sensible diet that is high in fruit and vegetables, you CAN enjoy the "naught treats" from time to time.

As long as you eat treats in moderation, there is nothing that is absolutely forbidden.

But moderation is the key.

Portions Sizes

In recent years portion sizes have grown enormously. Overeating as well as eating unhealthy foods are the two main factors in our epidemic of obesity.

This is also passed on to our children.

orry that their children are not eating enough when actually they are getting
ries than they need.

nt your child needs does depend on how active they are. Most toddlers are very
d that is great and should be encouraged. It also depends on size, gender and age.

You don't need to worry too much about exact portion sizes but it is interesting to look at
them to get a rough idea of how much food your toddler needs. You'd be surprised at how
little it is. I was surprised that recommendations say 1 biscuit a day rather than 1 packet of
biscuits a day!

An Average 2 Year Old Needs In 1 Day

Grains 2 ounces

Vegetables 1 cup

Fruit 1 cup

Dairy 2 cups

Protein 2 ounces

A "cup" is a standard unit of volume measurement of 240 mls or 8.45 imperial fluid ounces. It
can be quite confusing as some of the measurements are cups and some are weights, especially if you're used to using weights (as we do in the UK.) But if you think that an normal individual pot of yoghurt of 125 mls is roughly half a cup, it gives you an idea of what you're
aiming for. Half a cup of broccoli is as much cut up broccoli as you can fit into an empty yoghurt pot.

What exactly does that mean? What does it translate to in terms of actual food?

Grains. 1 oz of grains is 1 slice of regular bread, OR half a cup of cooked pasta or rice, OR 1
regular cookie OR half an english muffin OR 3 cups of popped pop corn OR 1 cup of breakfast cereal OR 1/2 cup of cooked oatmeal (porridge).

Vegetables. With most vegetables you can just cut them up and put them in a cup but lettuce
and leafy greens only count as half. One actual cup of lettuce counts as half a cup of vegetables in terms of your daily vegetable intake.

Fruit. Equally, you can just cut up most fruit and put it in the cup except dried fruit counts as
double. So you only need to eat half a cup of dried fruit to get one cup of fruit in terms of
your daily intake.

Dairy. The dairy section can be a little confusing. A cup of dairy could be 1 cup of milk OR half a cup of evaporated milk OR 1 cup of yoghurt OR 1/2 a cup of shredded cheese OR 2 ounces of processed cheese OR 2 cups of cottage cheese OR 1 cup of frozen yoghurt.

Protein 1 ounce of protein could be 1 egg OR 1 ounce of shell fish or fish OR 1 tablespoon of peanut butter OR 1/2 ounce of nuts or seeds OR 1/4 cup of cooked beans (black beans, kidney beans, pinto beans but NOT green beans) OR 1 ounce of cooked chicken, turkey, beef or pork OR 1 sandwich slice of turkey.

Menu Example

Breakfast 1/4 cup of cooked oatmeal (1/2 ounce of grains), 1 cup of milk in the oatmeal (1 cup of dairy)

Snack 1/2 cut up apple (1/2 a cup of fruit) and 1/2 cup of yoghurt (1/2 a cup of dairy)

Lunch 1/2 slice of bread (1/2 ounce of grains), 1 egg (1 ounce of protein) 1/2 cup of cherry tomatoes (1/2 cup of vegetables)

Snack 1/2 a biscuit (1/2 ounce of grains) 1 cup of frozen fruit yoghurt (1/2 cup of yoghurt, 1/2 cup of fruit)

Dinner 1/2 cup of broccoli (1/2 cup of vegetables) 1 ounce of meat sauce (1 ounce of protein) 1/4 cup of cooked pasta (1/2 cup grains)

Total Intake in 1 Day

Grains 2 ounces

Vegetables 1 cup

Fruit 1 cup

Dairy 2 cups

Protein 2 ounces

It gets complicated adding it all up doesn't it? But it is a good exercise to go through so that you can estimate how much your toddler actually eats compared to what the recommended amounts are.

It is much easier just to think in terms of proportions, so half is fruit and vegetables, a quarter is protein and a quarter is grains with a bit of dairy on the side.

In Summary

It's actually very easy to summarise a healthy diet.

Lots of fruit and vegetables. Less packets.

This is great news for us as it's actually very easy to add more fruit and vegetables to your kid's diet. There are many things that you don't even need to cook.

If you present your child with a serving of fruit or vegetables at every meal or snack time, you have gone a long way to helping them develop healthy eating habits.

But of course, you could offer them broccoli and cabbage every day but just sitting on the plate doesn't give them any health benefits. How are you actually going to get them to eat all that lovely healthy food?

In the next chapter we'll get to the nitty gritty. The "how to" bit. The "how to help your kids actually eat their veggies".

Chapter 4. What Every Parent Should Know About Milk and Toddlers

My cute two year old is sitting at the kitchen table. Surrounded by a giant puddle of milk. It's dripping off the table, onto the floor. A cheeky and triumphant smile on her face. She has managed to pour it herself. The fact that she has mostly missed the plastic cup doesn't deter her. "More Milk!" she barks. She will happily drink gallons of the stuff, whilst her twin won't even touch it.

Should I worry? Should I be concerned about how much milk my children drink? Like everything in life, it depends on many things.

How Much Milk Should My Child Drink?

1. Children over the age of one, should drink **mostly water**.

2. Milk is a great source of **calcium** which your kids need for their growing bones.

3. It's perfectly possible to get that calcium from other sources.

4. Children should drink **full fat milk** (unless otherwise advised by your doctor, dietician or nutritionist.)

5. They shouldn't be given semi-skimmed until they are two. Or skimmed until they are 5. Kids who eat a healthy diet are fine with full fat. Fat is good for their brains and helps them feel full. (Obviously this depends ALOT on the diet that your kids have. If you're not sure, discuss it with your family doctor.)

6. **Dairy sources** of calcium include yoghurt and cheese.

7. **Non-dairy** sources of calcium include canned fish that contain bones (the calcium is in the bones), soy beans and soy products such as soy milk, kale and some other leafy greens. (Your best bet is the fish and soy if you have young children and you actually want them to consume it.)

8. Children aged 2-3 need 2 cups of milk or equivalent. An example would be 1 cup of calcium-fortified soy milk and 1/2 a cup of shredded cheese.) A cup is 240 mls of liquid.

9. 1 cup of diary could be 1 cup of milk, 1 cup of yoghurt, 1 cup of calcium-fortified soy milk, 1 1/2 ounces of hard cheese or 2 cups of cottage cheese. Check out the conversions at MyPlate as it gets a little complicated.

10. Children aged 4-8 need 2 1/2 cups or equivalent.

11. Chocolate milk normally has lots of sugar in it. Think of it like a fizzy drink in terms of treats!

12. Cheese is very fatty and considered by MyPlate to be 'extra calories'. i.e. lots of calories with little nutritional benefit. To me, that translates as 'eat it in moderation'.

13. In my opinion, full fat cow's milk (or equivalent) is fine if you have a healthy diet. Follow-on formulas are an added expense.

What if my Kids don't Drink enough Milk?

You don't need to worry as long as they get their calcium from another source. They don't have to 'drink' it all. It's easy to get enough if you put it on your breakfast cereal or eat yoghurt or cheese. Or you can try other non-diary sources.

What if my Toddler drinks Loads of Milk?

That depends on exactly how much they are drinking. If their diet as a whole is balanced, they eat fruit and vegetables and get a bit from each food group, then it probably doesn't matter. The worry is that they drink only milk and then don't eat the other stuff. Go chat to your doctor if you're worried.

Now all I need to do is work on those pouring skills. Or make sure I put the milk away properly!

Chapter 5. Your Healthy Eating Routine

So now that you know that a healthy diet is one full of fruit and vegetables, you need to get your kids to actually eat those lovely healthy packets of goodness. How are we going to manage that?

With **patience** and **persistence**.

No Pressure

I mentioned it earlier, but pressuring your kids to eat is not the way to get them to eat. I know that we want our kids to be obedient and do as we say but we ALSO want them to grow up to have minds of their own. We want them to feel in control. We want them to learn to actually choose healthy foods. We want them to love healthy food.

Think about it.

If you were given a plate of worms to eat, you probably wouldn't be keen. If someone started to encourage you, would you be convinced? The more they start telling you how yummy they are, how you absolutely MUST try them, the more pressure they start putting on you, the more you back off and decide you don't want to.

Most people don't like being told what to do.

Children are no exception.

We are going to get out our best "I don't care what you eat" poker face. We are not going to let on that we REALLY REALLY REALLY want them to eat the broccoli.

We are going to pretend that we are indifferent.

We are going to let our kids make up their minds on their own.

Offer Healthy Food Throughout the Day

And here's the beauty of this system. If you offer your children healthy food throughout the day, guess what they're going to eat?

Yep! Healthy food.

You don't have to pressure them. They will eat SOMETHING.

Of course they might not eat exactly half of their diet as fruit and vegetables. They may eat a bit more carbohydrates or protein but we aren't going to worry. We will keep an eye on it and do things to encourage the vegetables but they will not be eating packets and packets of junk food.

Because we just aren't going to present them with junk food. (If that sounds scary, don't worry, I have some great tricks to help you present healthy food that I'll share later on.)

Regular Meal Times

Your healthy meal time routine is really easy. You just stick to your routine. A typical routine would be breakfast, snack, lunch, snack and then dinner.

The routine can vary slight to fit in with the comings and goings of your daily routine but you want to be offering your toddler healthy food every 2 and half to 3 hours.

Young children do not have the capacity to go long times in between eating times. (In fact, it's not great for adults either and if you skip a meal you normally end up by over compensating and eating whatever you can find later on. Generally something that comes out of a packet.)

I told you it was easy didn't I?

You offer healthy food, they decide if and what they want to eat.

No pressure. No fighting. No worries.

What if They Aren't Hungry?

If they aren't hungry, that's fine. We have to learn to trust our kids. We want them to eat when they are hungry and stop when they are no longer hungry. (Another reason why pressuring them isn't great as it teaches them to override the "I'm full up" signals.)

If they don't eat what you present, they will be hungry later and there will be another "healthy eating opportunity" in a few hours.

Moderate hunger isn't something to be feared.

Mix It Up

It is great to add variety to your kid's diet. The more variety that you offer them, the more likely they are to eat a healthy and varied diet. (It stands to reason really but is also backed up by research.)

But remember that they aren't going to eat anything new.

So mix up the healthy things that they do like with some new and strange things that they don't know. (You don't have to present new food all the time but frequently is a good idea.)

My Kids Don't Like Healthy

Many people claim that their kids only snack on cookies. They claim that they don't like healthy fruit or vegetables.

There is a simple solution. Stop offering them unhealthy food.

On Thursdays my oldest two boys do jujitsu, a marshall art after school. I offer them an extra snack as they won't eat dinner until later than normal.

Sometimes I bring them a treat, a chocolate biscuit. They gobble it up.

Other times I bring them fruit.

> *"I'm not hungry for a pear." They complain. "I'm only hungry for chocolate biscuits!"*

Which translates as "I'm not really hungry but I like chocolate biscuits and I'll eat them even when I'm not hungry."

If they were really and truly hungry, they would eat the fruit. There is no such thing as "only being hungry for junk food."

Dessert for Snack

You don't have to have dessert with every meal. In fact, I got so fed up of my kids "saving themselves" for dessert that I stopped them altogether. They would just refuse to eat dinner and only wanted dessert. Dessert was always healthy so on one hand it didn't matter but I didn't want my kids just skipping main course all the time.

So we stopped our healthy dessert of fruit and yoghurt and turned it into snack.

They still have the same food, it just has a different name. But at dinner time, they eat their meal if they are hungry rather than filling up on fruit.

On Friday and Saturday we still have dessert but I plan the meal as a "whole", the two courses together should make up the "My Plate" proportions.

Keep an Eye on What They Eat

I told you that you don't need to worry about what your kids eat but you do need to be aware of what they ACTUALLY eat. It's no good putting out lots of vegetable sticks that never get eaten.

But YOU are in control of what you offer.

I allow my kids to have up to one unhealthy treat a day. (Of course there are days when it's more such as when we go on holiday or a special occasion but equally there are days when they don't have an unhealthy treat.)

My idea of an "unhealthy treat" is anything that comes out of a packet. On an average day that would include cookies or biscuits as we call them. Sometimes, it would be more of a treat with a chocolate biscuit. At other times they may be allowed candy.

So. If they eat a healthy lunch and I can see that they have eaten a reasonable amount of vegetables, they will probably get a treat. I might bring them a chocolate biscuit after school before they go to jujitsu.

But. If they haven't touched their vegetables, they get a healthy snack of fruit and yoghurt. Or vegetable sticks and hummus.

You have the ability to modify what you offer them based on what they have eaten in the day.

Of course they don't know. I don't tell them because that would be pressuring them. I just want to ensure that whilst they are learning the rules for themselves they are also consuming a healthy diet.

Stop the Nagging for Snacks

If your child is constantly nagging for snacks, this method will put a stop to it. It may take a few days to get used to the routine, but once they have they will know when snack time is. When they ask for a snack, you simply tell them that they can have a snack at snack time which is in half an hour.

You have to make sure that you stick to your guns and aren't persuaded into letting them have an entire packet of cookies when you had planned to let them have fruit and yoghurt.

And of course you need to present healthy snacks. This system won't work if you offer healthy breakfast, lunch and dinner and then let them binge on packet food during snack time. They will simply fill up on junk when they can and refuse the healthy food. You need to offer healthy food at every meal and snack time.

If you're worried, I have some great tips to help you out. We'll get to them in a bit.

In Summary

So this is where we've got so far. You are going to offer your kids a healthy diet that is crammed full of fruit and vegetables. You aren't going to pressure them to eat but you are going to offer that healthy food at regular interval throughout the day and allow them to eat what they want out of the food that you offer.

Simple!

Now, I said that I have some extra tricks to help you out. A few ideas that will help you to ensure that your kids DO consume a healthy diet and continue to learn healthy eating habits. A few more bits and bobs...

Chapter 6. Some Other Bits and Bobs

So far we have got the basic structure of healthy eating by presenting healthy fruit and vegetables throughout the day but there are a few other tips and aims that I think are important to stress.

Remember that we are aiming to teach our children healthy eating habits. They won't get it immediately but we just have to be persistent.

Use a Knife and Fork or Spoon

If your kids are like mine, they would happily just pick up their food with their fingers and ram it in their mouths like little cave men. It is easy and when they are very little it is acceptable. But as they get older, they need to learn to use cutlery, not just for politeness sake.

With my older children who are perfectly capable of using a knife and fork, I find they often forget. I frequently make them just hold their knife so that when that instinct to use your hand occurs, they find their knife already there.

Eating slowly and smaller mouthfuls gives our body time to understand that it is full up. If you gulp down your meal in one bite, your brain doesn't understand that your tummy is full up and continues to feel hungry. This can lead us to overeat.

It's fine to give children help with cutting things up but they also need to practise this skill by themselves.

If they are really struggling, make a game of it and roll up some plasticine or play doh and practise cutting it up with a knife and fork.

Offer Fruit and Vegetables First

When your kids are hungry, use it to your advantage. Present them with the vegetables first. This may be in the form of a "starter" or "entree" but you could just leave a bowl of carrot sticks on the table and allow them to help themselves.

Family Meals

Kids learn by copying and family meals have been shown to be hugely advantageous in terms of healthy eating. In fact, not just healthy eating, your kids are more likely to behave well and perform better at school.

I know that it can be difficult with modern jobs and that often parents don't get back until after kids have finished eating. If that's the case, you can make use of the weekends to enjoy family meals and the person who is looking after the children at dinner time can still sit down and eat a small amount of food.

Model Good Behaviour

You cannot expect your kids to eat peas and carrots if you are sitting eating a packet of potato chips. If you love salad, they will learn to love salad. My daughter started eating lettuce when she was two. She'd just reach across and grab a bit out of the salad bowl. At first she'd chew it and spit it out. Now she's 3 and actually eats it.

She wants to be just like her mom and dad.

Buy Lots of Fruit and Vegetables

I know it sounds obvious but if you want to offer your kids a healthy diet, you need to buy healthy food. You need to buy lots of fruit and vegetables. If you're not sure where to start, go to a farmers market if you have one nearby. If not, go straight to the fruit and vegetable section at your supermarket and fill your trolley with healthy unprocessed food. (Stick to the outer aisles in the supermarket and avoid all the packages in the middle.)

Go for good quality fruit and vegetables that have a great taste and you won't need to do much to prepare them.

Other great things to buy include frozen or tinned fruit and vegetable and dried fruit and nuts. Choose packets that don't have any added sugar or salt or fat. You'd be surprised that sugar and oil are often added to dried fruit. Check the labels to find out.

Be strict when you buy your treats. If you don't buy loads, even if your kids nag for cookies you can't give them what you don't have.

Sit at the Table to Eat

In an ideal world, we would sit down at the table for every meal. We would eat our meal and when we had finished we would get down. Our meal is over.

Welcome to life with a toddler. My unruly daughter likes to get up, get down, get up again, get down again. Then she gets cross when I've cleared away the dinner things and her food is gone.

Sitting down to eat is good for our body. It helps us digest our food. It helps us concentrate on what we are eating.

If you are out and about, try to sit down to eat.

If you are at home and eating at the table, try to minimise coming and going. We want our children to learn to eat when they are hungry and stop when they are no longer hungry.

Don't Eat Watching TV

We want to concentrate on our food. To think about what we are eating. Mindless eating is a great way to learn to overeat because you aren't paying attention to your food. You are just eating out of habit.

Eat Until You are 80% Full

You don't need to eat until you're stuffed full of food. Teach your children to eat until they are no longer hungry. Or 80% full. Rather than bursting.

Small Plates and Small Servings

Serving food on a small plate makes it look like you have more food. It's a great trick for all of us. The same portion on a big plate looks like less so we have a tendency to over eat.

Children are often intimidated by too much food. It's better to give them a small portion and let them come back for more if they aren't full. In fact this is true for adults too as we are normally programmed to eat what is put in front of us.

Meal Plan

OK, I have a confession to make. I am totally incapable of writing up a week's meals. I know that the theory is great and there have even been studies that show that if you do it, you're more likely to cook healthy food.

I'm sure it isn't even that difficult. It's just not for me. But that doesn't mean that it's not for you. Half an hour one night a week will help you plan the week ahead and make sure you have healthy food for the rest of the week. And then you don't need to think about it any more.

Have Fruit On Sight

I know that we want to stick to our routine but if your kids simply can't wait for next meal and there is fruit sitting on the kitchen table, they will think of eating fruit.

It's not the end of the world if they eat an apple half an hour before dinner time. They may not eat as much vegetable pasta but they have still eaten something healthy.

Keep treats such as cookies and candy out of sight where they can't reach them. Of course they will ask for them, and quickly learn where they are kept, but they won't be able to help themselves.

Limit Pouches

I know that food pouches are easy and convenient and that many of them contain vegetables. However, they often have added fruit sauce which is naturally sweet so that kids don't get used to the taste of the vegetable by itself. They also don't teach children to recognise and choose vegetables.

Pouches have their place, but in moderation.

Playing with Food

Playing with food is a good way to familiarise kids with different food objects. You could play with actual food (preferably not the food they're supposed to be eating) or pretend food objects or pictures.

Toddler Appetites Fluctuate

Toddlers can be erratic eaters which is difficult if you are learning to trust them to choose what they want to eat. One day they will eat only apricots. The next only bread. One day they'll eat three bowls of lunch. The next day only three spoonfuls.

If you only look at what they eat in one meal, you're bound to worry that they are either overeating or undereating. Try to look at what they eat in an entire week rather than in one particular meal. It will give you a much better idea of their average consumption.

Toddler Diarrhoea

Toddler diarrhoea is very common. It is when you can see bits of undigested food, such as peas and sweetcorn in their poo. It is caused by them not chewing their food properly and isn't anything to worry about. If you are worried, or they have other symptoms, you should go to your doctor.

Choking Hazards

Children have much smaller windpipes (oesophagus or esophagus) than adults. If something gets stuck in your windpipe you will choke. Choking is the fourth leading cause of death in children under the age of 5 in the USA.

A child's oesophagus is approximately the width of a whole peanut so anything that size could potentially get stuck. Toddlers are not great at chewing. The risk is that you give them a lump of food and they swallow it whole but it's too large and gets stuck.

A simple solution is just to make sure the size of food that you present them is small enough to go down without a problem. For example, a whole grape may get stuck, but half a grape is fine. Equally whole nuts can be dangerous but crushed nuts on top of a cake are fine.

Foods To Avoid Due to Choking Hazard

- Whole grapes and cherry tomatoes

- Whole nuts and seeds

- Chunks of meat or cheese

- Hard or sticky candy

- Chunks of peanut butter

- Chunks of raw vegetables

- Chewing gum

- Hot dogs

- Pop corn

Toddlers, Naps and Eating Routine

Most toddlers nap during the day and it can seem complicated working out how to fit in so many naps, snacks and meals. Should they nap first or snack first?

Each child is different and will have their own unique rhythm to their day. My youngest, who are twins have totally different sleep requirements. Sebastian gave up his naps shortly after the age of 2 whereas his sister will happily still sleep 2 hours during the day. They're nearly 4 now.

So she will have her lunch, go for a nap and wake up in time for a snack (which she may or may not want to eat.)

It doesn't really matter which order you do it in as long as you are consistent and offer them food at regular intervals.

In Summary

Healthy eating habits are more than just what we eat. It is also important to pay attention as we eat, to eat slowly and to eat in a communal setting. That way we can help our body digest the food and learn to eat when we are hungry and stop when we are no longer hungry.

So now let's get on with preparing some actual food. Children need feeding every single day which can seem like an overwhelming chore. But I don't do Masterchef style cooking. I do simple, easy, healthy and tasty and I'll tell you how in the next chapter.

Chapter 7. Cooking Tips and Some Awesome Recipes

I know that cooking can sometime feel like a burden. But you know what? It's something we have to do (or someone has to do) every single day. Our kids need feeding and it's just as easy to provide them with healthy food when you know how as unhealthy food.

Change Your Mindset

Instead of thinking of cooking as an onerous duty, start to think of it as a relaxing family time. OK, I know, you have toddlers! Perhaps you can cook whilst they nap. You can enjoy the peace and quiet. Put on some music or the radio. Make it fun and enjoyable.

Or make it a sociable time. Get your kids involved. Yes, even toddlers can help cook. My son who is now 3 has been giving me cooking instructions since he was 2. He sits at the side of the hob and tells me which ring I need to put each pan on. He's normally right. Or he'll run off to retrieve the "laderwider" (aka a ladle) from his play kitchen when he realises I'll need it to make risotto.

Or your kids could sit and draw or write at the kitchen table.

And you know what? I'm not trying to encourage you to get drunk in charge of a toddler, but a small glass of beer isn't out of order.

Cooking is one of the foundations of family life. Food prepared with love tastes a billion times better than anything that comes out of a packet. Once you start enjoying cooking and eating as a family, everything else will fall into place.

Keep It Simple

You don't have to make it complicated. Those healthy vegetables that you bought just need a bit of cooking. You don't have to do anything elaborate unless of course you want to.

Vegetable pasta, vegetable chilli. Any simple meal with vegetables in it is a great place to start.

Cook Lots of Vegetables

If in doubt, double the amount of vegetables you're about to cook. Seriously.

Cook lots of different types and more than you expect people to eat. If they do eat them, great. If not, you can have them cold for lunch the next day. Drizzle them with good quality olive oil and call it a "Mediterranean Salad"!

Or whizz them up to make a soup.

Or freeze them.

Once you get into the habit of presenting lots of vegetables, you'll find that they never go to waste.

Present More Vegetables that You Expect Them To Eat

I'm talking different types of vegetables here. For example, if you offer carrots and your toddler is not in a carrot mood, they haven't eaten any vegetables. If you offer carrots and peas and they aren't in a carrot type of mood, perhaps they'll eat the peas. They have eaten a whole lot more vegetables than none.

The more different types you offer, the more chance you have of them eating some of the vegetables.

Good Quality Ingredients and Olive Oil

Buying good quality ingredients will save you hours of grief and effort. You don't need to turn them into a "dish", you can just cook them and let the flavours speak for themselves.

I may be biased by my Spanish friends but a drizzle of good quality olive oil is an amazing easy way to bring a plate of any vegetable to life. So easy and so quick!

Cooking With Kids

I have a photo of my 4 children, lined up in the kitchen "helping" me cook. Haha! I know parents dread those words "I want to help!" But even toddlers can start to help. Not only does it provide them essentially living skills and help them feel involved, it also gives them some control over what they eat.

Hiding Vegetables

Hiding vegetables so that children don't realise they are eating them is not a long term solution. If you give them spaghetti bolognese with lots of pureed vegetables in the sauce, it doesn't teach them to love those vegetables. But hiding vegetables does have its place. There are times when you do need to get healthy nutrients into your kids and if you have to hide them then that's what it takes. Just don't do it all the time. Make sure you present them with recognisable vegetables as well.

I also serve something such as soup that have whizzed up veggies. They aren't hiding as such, that's the recipe, but it's not apparent to the kids that they are in there unless of course you tell them.

In Summary

Homemade cooking is by far the best food to feed your family. It doesn't have to be complicated. Just use simple, clean, good quality ingredients and enjoy cooking and eating with your family.

In the next chapter I have a few of my most favourite and easy "recipes" or tricks that I use day in and day out to provide easy, healthy food that my kids love.

Chapter 8. Some Really Easy Recipes

This isn't a recipe book so I'm not going to include loads and loads of recipes BUT there a few really simple tricks that are worth knowing about. Simple recipes that will keep you in a stock of healthy meals and snacks without too much effort.

I like to keep my life simple!

Breakfast

Breakfast is a really important meal so don't be tempted to skip it. It sets us all up with energy that our bodies need to function throughout the day. For our kids that is brain power and energy to run around and have fun.

People who skip breakfast tend to overcompensate later on in the day.

Most people eat cereal out of a packet as it is very convenient. However, the vast majority of breakfast cereal is laden with added sugar and salt. Even the "healthy" type whole grain cereals have added sugar and salt. It drives me bonkers. Especially as it is so expensive.

You don't have to have cereal for breakfast. You can think entirely out of the box and go for vegetables, fruit and eggs. Or anything you like really.

But if you want to stick to a more traditional style breakfast there are a few things you can do to ensure your kids are getting the best start to the day.

Add Fruit

Either chopped up fruit or stewed fruit (we'll get to that shortly.) If you offer it every day, they may not eat it every day but they will eat it some days. Our favourite is cold baked peaches (no added sugar). It's like having dessert for breakfast.

Oats

Oats are great as they are a whole grain. They are also very versatile. You can make porridge (aka oatmeal) by cooking them up in some water or milk. It takes around 10 mins so not great if you're rushed in the morning but fine for the weekend or if you can manage to get up a little earlier.

You can be in control of how much sugar you add. We like honey (which is just a sugar substitute) or condensed milk (another sugar substitute). (Neither honey nor condensed milk are much healthier than normal sugar, they are just have a different taste. Both are very high in sugar but used sparingly that's fine.)

You can add a healthy topping of nuts, seeds, dried fruit, fresh fruit or stewed fruit. Or flavour it with a spice such as cinnamon.

Porridge is easy and very versatile.

The second easy recipe is **overnight oats**. In the UK we call it "Bircher muesli". It is very similar but saves you time in the morning. Many people find oats that have been soaked easier to digest.

Overnight oats take approximately 2 minutes to prepare. Add either water or milk (or yoghurt or cream if you like) and soak overnight. They are also very versatile. I normally start with whatever stewed fruit I have in the fridge but you can add fresh fruit, dried fruit or nuts. Again, anything you like really.

The last quick and easy recipe is homemade muesli. Simply combine a packet of oats with some dried fruit and nuts. (Make sure you buy packets with no added sugar or salt.) You can add fresh fruit too. So easy your kids can make it.

If you have bowls that the children have added milk to but haven't finished you can scrape it into your overnight oats. I told you nothing goes to waste!

Cooked Fruit

Cooked fruit is so easy and can be added to any meal you like. I buy fruit especially for cooking (normally the cheaper fruit that looks a bit battered but I know it will cook up fine.) You can also use any fruit that looks like it won't last much longer. (For us fruit doesn't last very long in the hot weather during summer, especially soft fruits.) And you can use the bits that are left over after your toddler has taken two bites of an apple and left the "core".

Stewed or Baked

You can either simmer it for 5 minutes on the hob with a cup full of water or you can bake it in the oven at 180°C (360°F) for 30-45 minutes depending on the size of the pieces and your oven. You'll know when it's done because it will be soft.

Our favourite is baked peaches. My kids love the juice so I add extra water to make more liquid but that's optional.

I also add a teaspoon of vanilla essence (the stuff that actually comes from the vanilla plant rather than the artificial flavouring.) Or cinnamon.

Stewed or baked fruit makes a delicious and healthy dessert.

But it's also great cold. Pop it in the fridge and use it whenever you like. You can add it to breakfast, or eat it as a healthy snack with yoghurt.

Salad

I love salad. In the summer I live off salad. Basically anything that I can chop up and chuck into a bowl. Lettuce, tomatoes, cucumber, celery, carrots, left over cold vegetables.

You can also add a little bit of protein such as some chopped up cheese, or cold sausage, nuts and seeds.

Even some stale bread crusts. You can turn them into croutons if you can be bothered but normally I just allow them to soak up the tomato juices and olive oil.

Every salad is different and you can tailor them to encourage your kids to eat something they like. If they pick out the carrots and the tomatoes to eat and leave the rest, that's great. Don't worry that they didn't touch the celery.

Different Dressings

You can add even more variety by playing around with dressings. The most basic (and very tasty) is just a drizzle of good quality olive oil and either some vinegar or lemon juice. Or just olive oil and a sprinkle of salt. If you want to make a typical french dressing, combine the olive oil, and acid (either vinegar or lemon juice) with a good dollop of good quality mustard. I like french dijon mustard but anything will do.

Salads are Easy and Forgiving

Salads are easy. You don't really need a "recipe". You just need to mix it all up. Just get on with it.

One of my favourite salads is grated carrot with a french dressing. I could eat it all day. And so could my 8 year old son (the one that is a bit fussy.) Or a simple tomato salad.

Soup

In the winter I replace my beloved salad with soup. It is equally easy although you do need to prepare it a bit ahead of time. Essentially I add lots of vegetables, some homemade stock and whizz it all up. It doesn't have to be complicated.

If you have cold left over vegetables, they transform into an easy soup that will take you 5 minutes to make. Chuck them in a pan, add your stock and whizz it up.

Homemade Stock

It sounds really difficult but it's really easy and is the base of many great recipes. You can use it to make soup, risotto or just add it to a meal that you are making for an extra burst of flavour.

Your basic ingredients are an onion, a carrot and some parsley and a bay leaf. You can also add other things, odds and ends that are left over. The stalk of the broccoli that you don't want to cook, the outside leaves of a cabbage or leeks that are too tough. Add a litre or 2 of water depending on how much you want to make (just cover the things that are in your pan.)

Simmer it all up for half an hour, drain it and keep it in the fridge. It will keep for around a week.

You can also make meat and fish stock. I sometimes use the left overs of a chicken to make chicken stock but generally I can't be bothered and find that vegetable stock is much easier and works just as well.

Chickpeas (Garbanzos), Legumes and Lentils

Chickpeas and lentils are a great source of plant protein. They are versatile and easy to cook. Lentils come in lots of different colours, red, green, brown, puy and legumes include all different types of dried beans such as chickpeas, black beans, white beans, haricot beans, canellini beans.

You can buy them pre cooked in either tins or jars. (Have a look to see what else they have added to the juice sometimes they add preserving agents and sugar and salt.) But they are convenient and I always rinse them to get rid of the liquid.

If you want to cook them from dried, you need to read the instructions. Most lentils don't need soaking and you can just add a handful to your pasta sauce. They cook in around 20 to

30 minutes. Most dried beans need to be soaked overnight, brought to the boil and then simmered. It is important to follow the instructions as some of them, such as red kidney beans are toxic if you don't cook them properly.

Easy Homemade Baked Beans

Baked beans is a childhood favourite and is actually a really easy meal to cook from scratch. Pick your favourite beans. I use a jar of chick peas and canellini beans (because that's what's available here.) Rinse them, add a tin of pureed tomatoes and a teaspoon of good quality smoked paprika. Done.

You can eat them for breakfast, lunch or dinner if you wish. OK in this house we are only allowed them for lunch otherwise my kids get upset that it's the wrong meal but in theory you could.

Top with a fried egg to make it extra delicious.

Homemade Hummus

Hummus is an amazing dip that originally comes from Lebanon. You can buy it ready made but it is normally expensive and often has lots of sugar and salt and other things added.

It's really cheap to make and only takes 5 minutes.

The basic ingredients are a tin of garbanzo beans, olive oil and water. You can also add garlic and tahini (sesame seed paste) if you want to be authentic but it's fine without. Just whizz them all up to the consistency that you want.

It's also very versatile and you can add different flavourings. An avocado, or a teaspoon of curry powder or cumin seeds.

The awesome thing about hummus is that is great to eat with vegetable sticks. Kids love dunking carrots sticks and gobbling it up. But you can present them with all manner of vegetable sticks. Don't worry if they don't try all of them.

Hummus is great for lunch or for a healthy snack.

Healthy Snacks

Snacks are a really important part of your healthy eating routine. But don't worry as you don't have to spend hours baking homemade muffins unless you want to.

Try to think of snacks as "mini meals". You want to think of the same proportions as the meals that you offer. That's half fruit and vegetables with a bit of protein and grains. Rather than all grains in the form of cookies and cake.

Fruit is an easy and healthy snack. You may want to add some yoghurt too. I use full fat yoghurt with no added sugar or salt. A little bit of fat is fine and helps us to feel full up and satisfied.

Dried nuts and dried fruit with no added sugar or salt are another easy and healthy snack.

Peanut butter is also another healthy alternative to shop bought cookies and cakes. (Again, look at the packet to make sure it doesn't have sugar or salt added.)

If you want to offer your children cookies, instead of offering the whole packet and letting them have free reign. Allow them to have one cookie and some fruit. You'd be surprised that sometimes they actually eat the fruit first.

In Summary

Healthy cooking is really easy when you know how and are in the habit. If you're not in the habit, don't worry, you'll get there. Pick one of these easy recipes and give it a go.

Conclusion

I hope that you now feel fully equipped to start on the amazing journey that is helping your kids to love healthy food. By teaching them healthy habits from an early age, you'll be reducing their risk of getting a whole host of nasty diseases later on in life.

Remember that you're going to offer your kids lots of healthy fruit and vegetables and less packet food that contains lots of added salt, sugar and other strange ingredients.

You're going to offer them healthy food in at regular intervals throughout the day. Your "healthy eating routine". You're going to allow them to decide what they want to eat, without pressuring them to eat food that they don't want to.

You're going to feel calm and relaxed as you know that they are learning healthy habits, that they aren't going to try new foods and that each individual pea doesn't matter. You are of course going to continue to offer them new and exciting foods, even though you know they won't eat them.

Gradually your kids will learn to eat and love a healthy diet and before you know it you'll have older kids who will gobble down healthy food.

To give you some encouragement, my oldest son who will be 8 in 2 days helped me cook dinner tonight. It was a pork curry with some coconut milk that I wanted to use up. I wasn't optimistic that it would be accepted (especially as I realised that I only had about 2 of the ingredients that I needed so we basically made it up). He ate two whole bowls, including the green beans. He left his courgettes (zucchini) but that's fine. He still ate a healthy meal without any fuss. And it was brand new!

Just keep going, keep presenting healthy food, some that is already accepted, some that is new. Keep going, continue to be patient and persistent and your kids will not only learn to love healthy food, they will learn to choose healthy food.

They will learn healthy habits that they will keep until adulthood and hopefully they'll pass them onto their children too. What an amazing thought!

I hope you've loved this book as much as I have loved writing it. I really do passionately think that the key our obesity epidemic is to teach our children to eat healthily and to form healthy habits early on in life.

I do understand that many people need extra help, they might need the help of a community or a coach so I have included a page about my awesome resources.

But before we get to that, I have a huge favour to ask of you. You would really be helping me out if you could leave a **review** on amazon.

Please Review This Book

If you love this book, please leave a review on amazon. It will help to reach other people like you who are struggling to feed their toddlers a healthy diet.

Thank you so much! Reviews are really important to me and I'm really grateful that you've taken the time to leave one.

Resources

If you'd live more help with helping your children to eat healthy food, I have heaps of resources on my site, https://snotty-noses.com.

I have lots of free guides to help you. You can find them all on the "resource" page. You just need to sign up to my newsletter to receive the free gift and then you can access all of them.

Healthy Eating Free Resources

Help Your Picky Eater

Help Your Kids Love Healthy Food

How to Introduce Kids to New Foods

Introducing Your Baby To Solid Foods

Healthy Snacks for Kids

Healthy Toddler Diet

Free Video Course

Bite Size Video Course

Free Baby Resources

How to Teach Your Baby to Sleep (with foreword by world sleep expert Professor Fleming.)

What to Do When Your Baby is Unwell

Healthy Eating for Children Video Course

Now that you've read this book, you have the foundation, the "theory" to feed your child a healthy diet.

But lots of people need MORE help. They need to have some reminders, some nudges, some extra encouragement to make those changes.

Changing habits can be tough but I"m here to help!

The **Snotty Noses Healthy Eating for Children Course** will help you instil healthy eating habits without the stress.

> *"Orlena understands first-hand the frustrations of getting kids to eat healthily. Her brilliant course will not only give you plenty of practical advice you can use immediately with your fussy eaters, but will probably get your whole family eating better!"*

Anne, The Gingerbread Mum

Find out more https://snotty-noses.com/healthy-eating-course/.

Private Coaching

Some people like to have a personal, tailored to their family approach.

If that is you, I offer personal, private coaching to address your individual worries and concerns.

If you'd like to learn more, check out http://snotty-noses.com/shop/coaching.html.

Or email me directly at orlena@snotty-noses.com

Good bye

Congratulations on getting to the end of the book. I hope that you feel equipped to teach your children to love and enjoy healthy food.

Please keep in contact, I love to hear from readers and if you ever need any extra help, feel free to pop over and say hello.

Orlena

Made in the USA
San Bernardino, CA
18 December 2019

61887957R00031